My Spelling Workbook

Prim-Ed
Publishing

Prim-Ed Publishing would like to thank the teachers and pupils from the following schools for their assistance in the production of this *My Spelling Workbook* programme:

Merrylee Primary School, Glasgow

Balbardie Primary School, West Lothian

Brackens Primary School, Dundee

Braehead Primary School, Dumbarton

East Fulton Primary School, Renfrewshire

Knockburn Primary School, Glasgow

Pitfour Primary School, Aberdeenshire

Saracen Primary School, Glasgow

St. Catherine's Primary School, Glasgow

The Mary Russell School, Renfrewshire

Woodlands Primary School, Renfrewshire

My Spelling Workbook – Book D
© Prim-Ed Publishing

Offices in: United Kingdom: PO Box 2840, Coventry, CV6 5ZY
Australia: PO Box 332, Greenwood, Western Australia 6924
Republic of Ireland: Bosheen, New Ross, Co. Wexford, Ireland

Published in 2003 Prim-Ed Publishing
ISBN 1 86400 764 8

Introduction

Welcome to *My Spelling Workbook*. This book has lots of different activities to help you improve your spelling. Here are some tips to show you the best way to use your book.

- **Learning Words**

  Each list of words in the book has two practise columns to write the words. There is also a column for your teacher to tick if you get your dictation correct. Any words which you spell wrongly can be added to the 'Difficult Words I Have Found' table. You can also add any difficult words you find.

- **Look, Say, Cover, Write, Check**

  These words are to remind you of the best way to learn to spell. You should follow this when you are learning each word. Use the flap to cover the list words when you practise them.

- **Recording your Scores**

  At the back of the book, you will find a grid for recording your scores for each unit. This will help you to keep track of how you are improving with your spelling.

- **How to Become a Better Speller**

  1. *Have a go!*
     Write the word on the piece of paper.
     Does it look right? If it doesn't look right, try writing it another way.

  2. *Look around your classroom*
     There are probably many words around you that you just didn't notice.

  3. *Use a dictionary*
     Try using a dictionary before you ask a teacher.

  4. *Ask the teacher*
     If you have tried the first three, then ask a teacher for help.

Contents

Revision Unit 1 2–3

Unit 1 4–5

Unit 2 6–7

Unit 3 8–9

Unit 4 10–11

Unit 5 12–13

Unit 6 14–15

Unit 7 16–17

Unit 8 18–19

Revision Unit 2 20–21

Unit 9 22–23

Unit 10 24–25

Unit 11 26–27

Unit 12 28–29

Unit 13 30–31

Unit 14 32–33

Unit 15 34–35

Unit 16 36–37

Revision Unit 3 38–39

Unit 17 40–41

Unit 18 42–43

Unit 19 44–45

Unit 20 46–47

Unit 21 48–49

Unit 22 50–51

Unit 23 52–53

Unit 24 54–55

Revision Unit 4 56–57

Unit 25 58–59

Unit 26 60–61

Unit 27 62–63

Unit 28 64–65

Unit 29 66–67

Unit 30 68–69

Unit 31 70–71

Unit 32 72–73

Revision Unit 5 74–75

My Dictionary Words 76–78

Revision Unit 1

List Words	Practise	Practise	D
June			
August			
September			
December			
love			
same			
England			
France			
Germany			
Spain			

All Mixed Up

1. Unjumble these revision words. Some of the letters may be capitals.

   (a) s t u g u a _____

   (b) c a r n e f _____

   (c) a p i n s _____

   (d) e m a s _____

   (e) v o l e _____

   (f) b r e m e d e c _____

Small Words

2. Find smaller words in these words.

   (a) Germany _____

   _____

   _____

   _____

   _____

   (b) England _____

   _____

   _____

   _____

3. Find and circle these words in the story.

same	June
August	September
December	love
England	France
Germany	Spain

We have had the (same) holidays in June and August to France and Germany for years. I would love instead to go to England in September and Spain in December.

Missing Words

4. Complete, using the revision words.

(a) We are going to _____ in _____.

(b) I would _____ to come to _____ with you.

(c) We have the _____ birthday in _____.

(d) We flew from _____ to _____.

Word Worm Anagram

5. Choose every third letter and then rearrange them to make a list word.

k l e b h m v f s w e p n m e z x r p l b u i e g h t

Word Hunt

6. (a) Which words name countries? _____ _____

_____ _____

(b) Which words name months? _____ _____

_____ _____

(c) Which words end in a vowel? _____ _____

_____ _____

List Words	Practise	Practise	D
chuckle			
prickle			
tickle			
buckle			
tackle			
pickle			
crackle			
speckle			
apple			
yellow			

Synonyms

1. Find a list word with a similar meaning.

   (a) giggle _____

   (b) dot _____

   (c) attempt _____

   (d) clasp _____

Adding Endings

2. Complete this table of suffixes.

(a) tickle		
(b)	buckled	
(c) pickle		
(d) tackle		
(e)		chuckling

Revision Words

whether   stalk   merry   twice   wand   lost

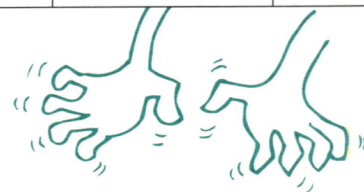

Difficult words I have found	Practise	Practise

3. Use list and revision words to solve the crossword.

Across

2. Rhymes with tickle and pickle.
7. Touch to make someone laugh.
8. I will do it _____ you like it or not.
10. A small dot.
13. Wood makes this noise on the fire.
14. Laugh.
15. A magic stick.

Down

1. A fruit.
3. Opposite of found.
4. Get going at a task.
5. Jolly.
6. Two times.

9. The colour of an egg yolk.
11. You make this by leaving it in vinegar.
12. This fastens a belt.

Missing Letters

4. Complete the list word and write it.

(a) __ p __ __ __   _____

(b) __ p e __ __ __ __   _____

(c) c __ a __ __ __ __   _____

(d) __ h __ c __ __ __   _____

Word Worm

6. Cross out every second letter. The leftover letters will make three list or revision words.

Alphabetical Order

5. Write these words in alphabetical order.

yellow   apple   prickle   pickle

(a) _____

(b) _____

(c) _____

(d) _____

List Words	Practise	Practise	D
example			
simple			
pimple			
couple			
handle			
doodle			
needle			
cuddle			
another			
does			

All Mixed Up

1. Unjumble the list words.

   (a) p s l m i e   _____

   (b) s o e d   _____

   (c) l e m p i p   _____

   (d) h e r a n o t _____

Revision Words

whisper

sulk

funny

ice

doom

abyss

Word Meanings

2. Match the words to their meanings.

   (a) doom •   • easy

   (b) simple •   • pair

   (c) couple •   • hug

   (d) cuddle •   • fate

Difficult words I have found	Practise	Practise

3. Find these list and revision words in the word search.

e	x	a	m	p	l	e	q	w	w
t	r	c	o	u	p	l	e	h	e
y	u	i	c	e	l	p	m	i	p
i	o	p	l	e	n	m	k	s	a
h	a	n	d	l	e	i	f	p	n
a	m	o	o	d	e	s	u	e	o
b	s	e	o	d	d	u	n	r	t
y	g	h	d	u	l	l	n	j	h
s	f	d	l	c	e	k	y	s	e
s	b	v	e	e	c	x	z	a	r

handle	example
doodle	simple
needle	couple
cuddle	pimple
does	another
whisper	sulk
funny	ice
doom	abyss

Small Words

4. Find small words in these list words.

(a) handle _____ _____ _____

(b) another _____ _____ _____ _____

_____ _____ _____

(c) example _____ _____ _____ _____

(d) needle _____

Mixed Up Sentences

5. Unjumble the sentences.

(a) chin. have You another on pimple your

_____

(b) me example a rhyme. Give an simple of

_____

(c) doom fell met He when in his abyss. the he

_____

List Words	Practise	Practise	D
plane			
plain			
waist			
waste			
steel			
steal			
check			
cheque			
well			
large			

Letters into Words

1. Write three list words using the letters on the plane.

   _____

   _____

   _____

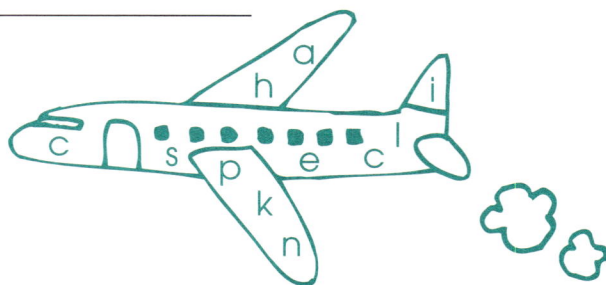

Revision Words

whale	folk
chess	soon
frost	room

Changing Words

2. Change one letter in each word to make a list word.

   (a) steam _____

   (b) plant _____

   (c) taste _____

   (d) chick _____

   (e) barge _____

Difficult words I have found	Practise	Practise

3. Use list and revision words to solve the crossword.

Across

2. Your middle.
4. Spoil.
6. We can fly in this.
7. Big.
9. Fit.
10. This is cold.
13. Make sure.
14. Not fancy.

Down

1. Write one of these to pay.
3. A strong metal.
4. A sea mammal.
5. Take what is not yours.
8. A place in a house.
10. People.

11. In a short time.
12. A board game.

Rhyming Words

4. Choose two words from the list to rhyme with:

    (a) speck _____ _____

    (b) chain _____ _____

    (c) heal _____ _____

Word Hunt

5. (a) Which list word has the letters 'qu' in it?

        _____

    (b) Which word means the opposite to small?

        _____

Homophones

6. Circle and write the correct word.

    (a) Tie the safety rope round your waste/waist.   _____

    (b) Cheque/Check whether the baby is sleeping or not.   _____

    (c) He flew the plane/plain over the Alps.   _____

    (d) The suspension bridge is made of steal/steel.   _____

List Words	Practise	Practise	D
grumble			
tumble			
crumble			
double			
stumble			
Bible			
able			
table			
must			
train			

Adding Endings

1. Complete this table of suffixes.

(a) grumble		
(b)		crumbling
(c)	stumbled	
(d) double		

Small Words

2. Write the list word that contains these small words.

(a) in _____

(b) us _____

(c) do _____

(d) rum _____

_____

(e) tab _____

Revision Words

while   silk   silly   face   swan   compost

Difficult words I have found	Practise	Practise

3. Find these list and revision words in the word search.

grumble   tumble

stumble   double

crumble   Bible

able   table

must   train

while   silk

silly   face

swan   compost

s	i	l	l	y	e	l	b	u	o	d
m	n	e	b	v	c	x	z	a	s	w
g	f	l	t	u	m	b	l	e	d	h
h	j	b	s	t	k	s	i	l	k	i
u	c	m	u	a	e	i	o	p	l	l
g	r	u	m	b	l	e	y	t	r	e
s	u	t	x	l	b	z	a	q	w	e
w	m	s	e	e	i	d	c	f	v	f
a	b	l	e	t	B	s	w	a	n	r
g	l	t	s	o	p	m	o	c	b	n
j	e	t	r	a	i	n	u	e	y	h

Secret Words

4. (a) Change the 'tr' to 'p' in train.

_____

(b) Change the 'm' to 'j' in must.

_____

(c) Change the 'd' to 'tr' in double.

_____

Word Challenge

5. Make as many words as you can from letters in this word.

stumble

_____

_____

_____

Missing Words

6. Complete using one of the list or revision words.

train   grumble   compost   crumble   table   silk   while   able

(a) Don't _____ when you're asked to set the _____.

(b) The bride's _____ is made of _____.

(c) Are you _____ to spread the _____ on the flower bed?

(d) You _____ the cheese _____ I heat the milk.

List Words	Practise	Practise	D
paste			
taste			
baste			
caste			
patch			
hatch			
catch			
match			
even			
such			

Change the Tense

1. Change the list words to past tense.

	Past	Present
(a)	waste	wasted
(b)	baste	_____
(c)	taste	_____
(d)	paste	_____

Revision Words

bless

whirl

walk

jelly

price

warn

Rhyming Words

2. Choose a rhyming word from the list or revision words.

(a) much _____

(b) last _____

(c) haste _____

(d) latch _____

(e) dawn _____

Difficult words I have found	Practise	Practise

3. Use list and revision words to solve the crossword.

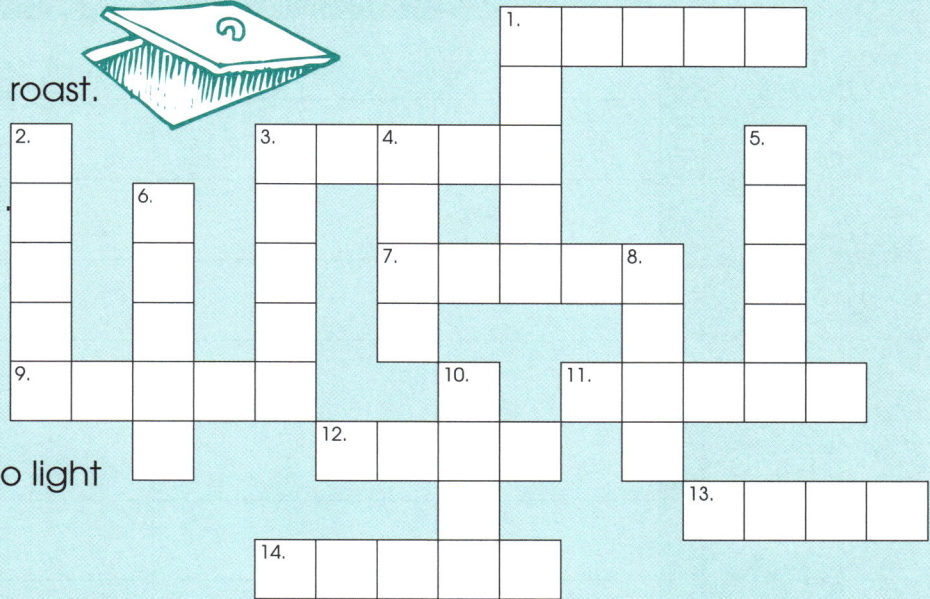

Across

1. Put hot fat over a roast.
3. Stick on.
7. Rhymes with 'last'.
9. Trapdoor.
11. Wobbly sweet.
12. Alert to danger.
13. Take steps.
14. You can use this to light the fire.

Down

1. To make holy.
2. If I throw it, will you _____ it?
3. A bit of cloth to cover a hole.
4. I have _____ a sore head.
5. Spin.
6. Sample food.
8. Not odd.
10. Cost.

Secret Code

4. Use the secret code to find out the list or revision word.

(a) __ __ __ __ __
 13 4 5 9 7

(b) __ __ __ __ __
 8 1 10 11 3

(c) __ __ __ __
 13 1 7 6

(d) __ __ __ __
 10 12 2 4

(e) __ __ __ __ __
 8 9 5 2 3

(f) __ __ __ __ __
 11 1 10 11 3

a	c	e	h	i	k	l	p	r	s	t	u	w
1	2	3	4	5	6	7	8	9	10	11	12	13

Proof-reading

5. Circle the incorrect words and rewrite them on the lines.

(a) I must warn/warm you that the prise/price is high.

_____ _____

(b) Paste/Paist that patsh/patch over the hole in the wall.

_____ _____

List Words	Practise	Practise	D
uncle			
article			
cycle			
icicle			
bicycle			
obstacle			
miracle			
particle			
because			
turn			

Missing Letters

1. Complete the list word and write it.

   (a) __ n __ __ __ _____

   (b) __ u __ n _____

   (c) i __ i __ __ e _____

   (d) __ y c __ __ _____

Revision Words

access   wash   whip   talk   wall   post

Alphabetical Order

2. Write these words in alphabetical order.

   obstacle   bicycle

   miracle   because

   (a) _____

   (b) _____

   (c) _____

   (d) _____

Difficult words I have found	Practise	Practise	

3. Find these list and revision words in the word search.

uncle	article
cycle	icicle
bicycle	obstacle
miracle	particle
because	turn
access	wash
whip	talk
wall	post

q	w	m	h	s	a	w	e	r	t	o
o	t	i	i	u	y	t	s	o	p	b
e	a	r	p	w	h	i	p	l	k	s
s	l	a	r	t	i	c	l	e	j	t
u	k	c	h	u	g	i	l	f	s	a
a	z	l	a	r	s	c	a	d	s	c
c	x	e	c	n	v	l	w	b	e	l
e	c	l	v	b	n	e	m	n	c	e
b	i	c	y	c	l	e	x	z	c	a
d	s	y	e	l	c	i	t	r	a	p
u	n	c	l	e	f	w	e	c	v	b

Mixed Up Sentences

4. Unjumble the sentences.

   (a) difficult climb. wall obstacle The a to was

   _____

   (b) my newspaper. the in about Talk article the uncle to

   _____

Word Meanings

5. Match the words to their meanings.

   (a) miracle •   • a very small piece of something

   (b) turn •   • the right to enter

   (c) particle •   • a surprising and amazing event

   (d) access •   • a brother of your mum or dad

   (e) uncle •   • move in a different direction

Letters into Words

6. Write three list words using the letters on the icicle.

   _____

   _____

   _____

List Words	Practise	Practise	D
twiddle			
fiddle			
muddle			
middle			
bubble			
stubble			
hobble			
rubble			
nothing			
pretty			

Synonyms

1. Find a list word with a similar meaning.

   (a) limp _____

   (b) bristles _____

   (c) attractive _____

   (d) centre _____

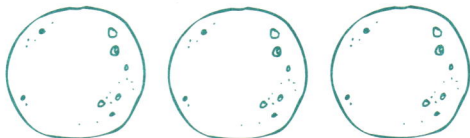

Revision Words

cress

story

race

watch

moon

host

Secret Words

2. (a) Change the 'tw' to 'r' in twiddle.

   _____

   (b) Change the 'no' to 'some' in no⁻hing.

   _____

   (c) Change the 'pr' to 'j' in pretty.

   _____

Difficult words I have found	Practise	Practise

3. Use list and revision words to solve the crossword.

Across

4. Centre.
6. Zero.
7. Tale.
9. Do this with your thumbs.
14. Limp.
15. You might find this on a man's chin.
16. Mix up.

Down

1. Attractive.
2. You see this in the sky at night .
3. The person giving the party.
5. Violin.
8. Run to win.
10. It tells the time.
11. A bit of broken stone.

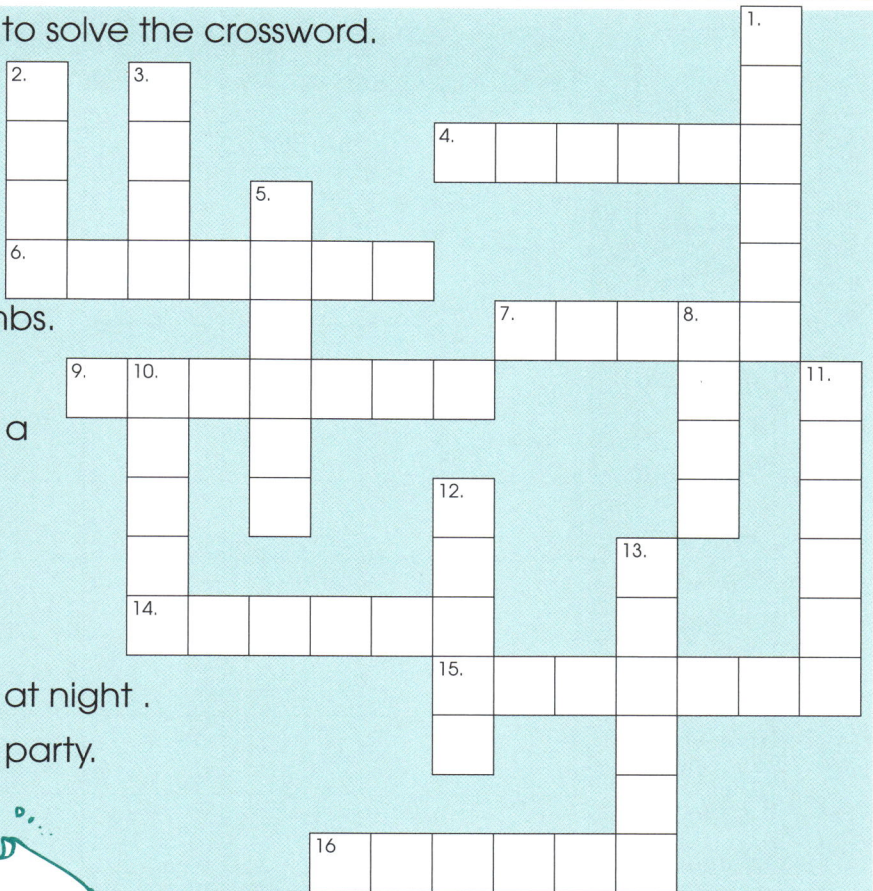

12. Egg and _____ sandwich.
13. You can blow one.

Adding Endings

4. Complete this table of suffixes.

(a) bubble		
(b)	raced	
(c)		hobbling
(d) fiddle		

All Mixed Up

5. Unjumble the list words.

(a) b l u b e b _____

(b) n i n g t h o _____

(c) l e b r u b _____

(d) t y r p e t _____

Memory Master

6. Cover the list and revision words. Write two from memory.

_____   _____

Write a sentence using both words.

_____

List Words	Practise	Practise	D
brittle			
bottle			
nettle			
settle			
kettle			
cattle			
battle			
rattle			
ask			
went			

Change the Tense

1. Change the tense of the list words.

Present	Past
(a) ask	asked
(b) settle	_____
(c) battle	_____
(d) _____	went

Small Words

2. Write the list words that contain these small words.

(a) as _____

(b) it _____

(c) set _____

(d) we _____

(e) at _____ _____

_____

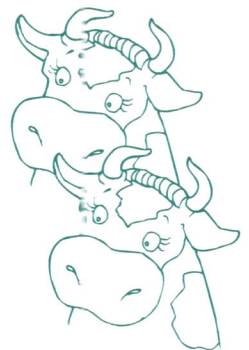

Difficult words I have found	Practise	Practise

3. Find these list and revision words in the word search.

brittle	bottle
nettle	settle
kettle	cattle
battle	rattle
ask	went
kiss	hurry
mice	cost
zoom	boon

z	d	s	n	o	o	b	h	j	z	k
x	m	a	y	u	r	e	g	k	x	e
c	o	t	k	i	s	s	w	e	n	t
v	o	s	t	i	t	e	f	e	c	t
b	z	o	r	c	a	t	t	l	e	l
m	i	c	e	o	y	t	d	t	v	e
n	f	q	l	p	u	l	s	t	b	l
m	b	o	t	t	l	e	a	a	n	t
l	g	w	t	o	i	w	q	r	m	t
k	k	s	a	y	r	r	u	h	l	e
j	h	e	b	r	i	t	t	l	e	n

Word Challenge

4. Make as many words as you can from letters in this word.

   battle

   _____

   _____

   _____

Word Hunt

5. (a) Which two revision words have double 'o'?

   _____ _____

   (b) Which list word starts with two consonants?

   _____

Revision Words

kiss   hurry   mice   cost   zoom   boon

Missing Words

6. Complete using one of these list or revision words.

   kiss settle Ask battle cattle brittle cost Hurry

   (a) _____ if this shop sells _____ toffee.

   (b) The _____ to win the stretch of land _____ a great deal.

   (c) _____ and _____ Grandma goodnight.

   (d) The _____ will _____ in that field for the night.

List Words	Practise	Practise	D
does			
must			
nothing			
yellow			
another			
large			
such			
because			
pretty			
went			

All Mixed Up

1. Unjumble these revision words.

   (a) w l e o y l _____

   (b) n e w t _____

   (c) h e r t o n a _____

   (d) i n t o h g n _____

   (e) t y e r t p _____

   (f) g a r e l _____

Small Words

2. Find smaller words in these words.

   (a) yellow _____

   _____

   (b) must _____

   (c) does _____

   _____

Word Worm

3. Circle four revision words which are written backwards in the word worm.

   h r e h t o n a c e g r a l v y t t e r p t e s u a c e b j

4. Find and circle these words in the story.

must ✓	large
does	such
nothing	because
yellow	pretty
another	went

I (must) plant another row of large, yellow flowers, because nothing does such a good job of hiding the missing post where the dog went through and dug up the pretty garden next door.

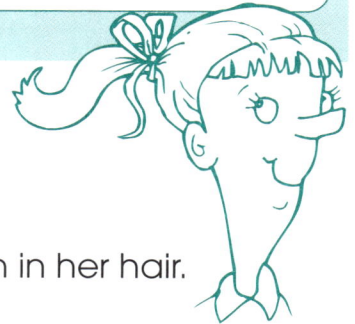

Missing Words

5. Complete, using the revision words.

(a) The _____ girl wore a _____ ribbon in her hair.

(b) I am so thirsty I _____ have a _____ glass of water.

(c) I _____ to bed _____ I was tired.

(d) It was _____ a _____ lawn it took three hours to mow.

Word Hunt

6. (a) Which three words are adjectives?

_____ _____

_____

(b) Which word means the opposite to 'small'?

_____

(c) Which two words have the word 'no' in them?

_____ _____

No-oo-o!

List Words	Practise	Practise	D
wriggle			
giggle			
toggle			
goggle			
nozzle			
guzzle			
ripple			
cripple			
friend			
read			

Rhyming Words

1. Choose a rhyming word from the list.

   (a) boggle _____

   (b) muzzle _____

   (c) trend _____

   (d) stipple _____

Word Worm

2. Use every third letter to make two list words.

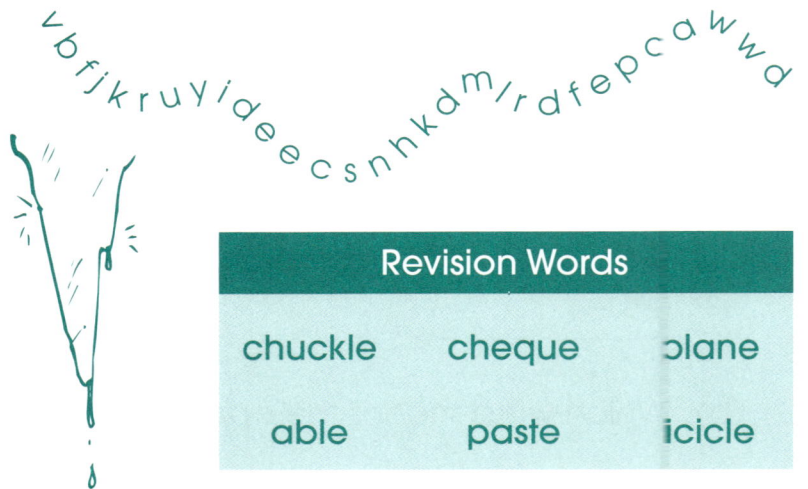

v b f j k r u y i d e e c s n h k d m l r d f e p c a w w d

Revision Words

chuckle	cheque	plane
able	paste	icicle

Difficult words I have found	Practise	Practise

3. Use list and revision words to solve the crossword.

Across

3. Skilful.
7. Laugh.
8. Eat greedily.
10. Stare wide-eyed.
11. Squirm.
14. Disable.
15. Do this with a book.

Down

1. Glue.
2. A frozen drip of water.
4. A spout on a hose.
5. Write one to pay.
6. You fly in this.
8. A nervous laugh.

9. A bar-shaped button.
12. Small wave.
13. Pal.

Secret Code

4. Use the secret code to find out the list or revision word.

(a) __ __ __ __ __ __
    5 13 8 4 11 3

(b) __ __ __ __ __
    12 1 14 15 4

(c) __ __ __ __ __ __
    13 8 12 12 10 4

(d) __ __ __ __ __ __ __
    17 13 8 6 6 10 4

a	c	d	e	f	g	h	i	k
1	2	3	4	5	6	7	8	9

l	n	p	r	s	t	u	w
10	11	12	13	14	15	16	17

Adding Endings

5. (a) Add 'ing' to these words.

giggle   giggling

guzzle   _____

ripple   _____

wriggle   _____

(b) What happens when you add 'ing'?

_____

_____

_____

_____

List Words	Practise	Practise	D
subtract			
multiply			
divide			
kilometre			
millimetre			
circle			
rectangle			
pentagon			
add			
land			

Symbols

1. Write the correct word for these symbols.

(a) _____

(b) _____

(c) _____

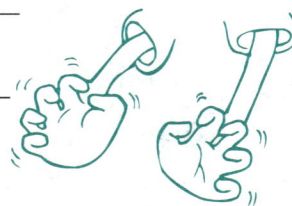

Letters into Words

2. Write three list words using the letters on the pentagon.

_____

_____

_____

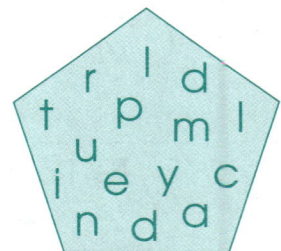

Revision Words

stubble   steal   tickle   cuddle   tumble   waist

Difficult words I have found	Practise	Practise

3. Find these list and revision words in the word search.

d	i	v	i	d	e	d	n	a	l	m
d	m	c	x	t	p	e	o	t	e	i
a	t	v	z	u	l	l	i	i	l	l
t	s	c	a	m	k	c	u	c	b	l
c	i	u	s	b	j	r	y	k	b	i
a	a	d	y	l	p	i	t	l	u	m
r	w	d	d	e	h	c	t	e	t	e
t	n	l	f	g	l	a	e	t	s	t
b	p	e	n	t	a	g	o	n	r	r
u	b	k	i	l	o	m	e	t	r	e
s	e	l	g	n	a	t	c	e	r	e

- subtract
- multiply
- divide
- kilometre
- millimetre
- circle
- rectangle
- pentagon
- add
- land
- stubble
- steal
- tickle
- cuddle
- tumble
- waist

Word Meanings

4. Write the list or revision word that matches each meaning.

(a) a unit of length equal to one thousandth of a metre. _____

(b) a shape with five sides _____

(c) to increase in number _____ _____

Secret Words

5. (a) Change the 'sub' to 'at' in subtract.

_____

(b) Change the 'mill' to 'cent' in millimetre.

_____

(c) Change the 'pent' to 'hex' in pentagon.

_____

Read and Draw

6. (a) Draw a pentagon.
(b) Draw a rectangle inside the pentagon.
(c) Draw a circle inside the rectangle.

List Words	Practise	Practise	D
decline			
decide			
declare			
deluxe			
depart			
detach			
descend			
deprive			
different			
home			

Missing Letters

1. Complete the list word and write it.

   (a) __ __ s c __ __ __   _____

   (b) __ __ __ e   _____

   (c) d __ __ __ x __   _____

   (d) __ __ f f __ __ __ __   _____

Change the Tense

2. Change the tense of the list words.

Present	Past
(a) depend	depended
(b) detach	_____
(c) descend	_____
(d) depart	_____

PLAIN flour

Revision Words

baste   rubble   obstacle   tackle   handle   plain

Difficult words I have found	Practise	Practise

3. Use list and revision words to solve the crossword.

Across

3. Manage.
4. Leave.
6. Not the same.
8. Stitch.
9. Separate.
11. Barrier.
13. Speak out.
15. Take away.
16. Make up your mind.

Down

1. Refuse.
2. Go down.
5. Broken stone.
7. Attempt.   12. Not fancy.
10. Where you live. 14. Luxury.

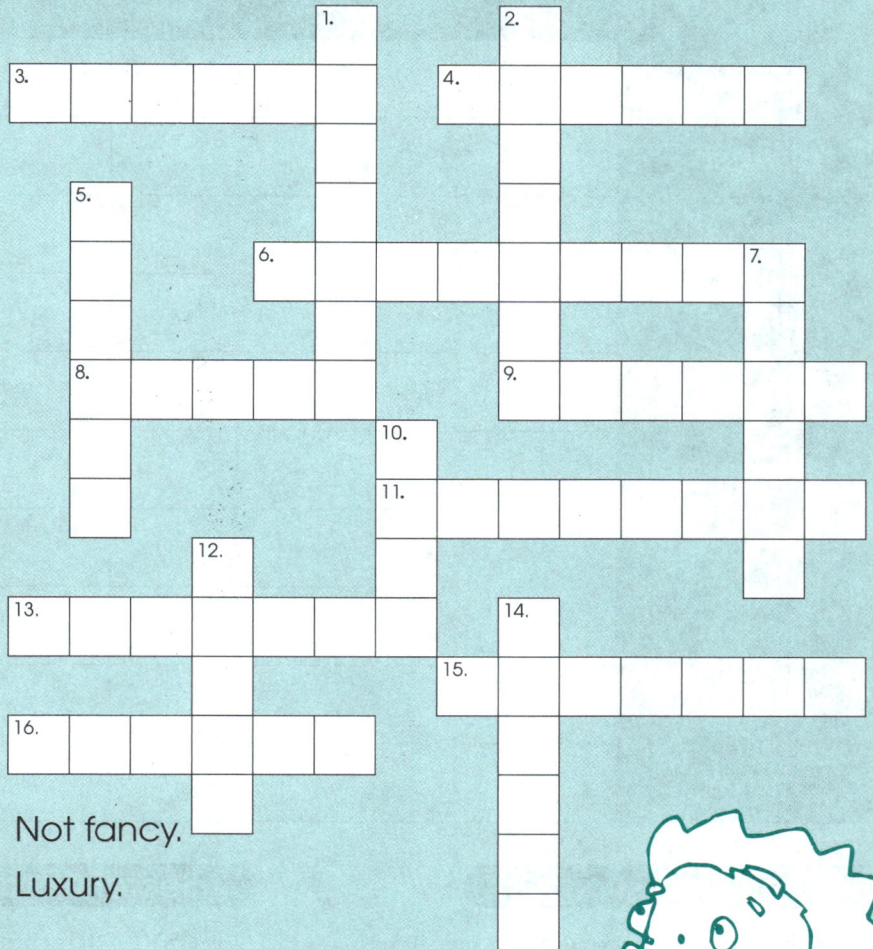

Missing Words

4. Complete using one of these list or revision words.

> obstacle   decline   different   decide   depart   rubble

(a) He may _____ to _____ your invitation.

(b) The fallen _____ caused an _____ on the path.

(c) The ship will _____ for a _____ port at noon.

Mixed Up Sentences

5. Unjumble the sentences.

(a) hands you food. Wash before handle the your

_____

(b) a We holiday. in villa deluxe on stayed

_____

List Words	Practise	Practise	D
disaster			
disease			
distract			
discover			
dispose			
disagree			
disappoint			
disgust			
us			
move			

Synonyms

1. Find a list word with a similar meaning.

   (a) argue _____

   (b) sickness _____

   (c) find _____

   (d) shift _____

Secret Words

2. (a) Change the 'dis' to 'at' in distract.

   _____

   (b) Change the 'dis' to 'un' in discover.

   _____

   (c) Change the 'dis' to 'gr' in disease.

   _____

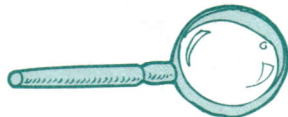

Difficult words I have found	Practise	Practise	

3. Find these list and revision words in the word search.

disaster	disease
distract	discover
dispose	disagree
disappoint	disgust
us	move
simple	double
particle	example
twiddle	nettle

d	m	f	e	l	c	i	t	r	a	p
i	n	d	t	w	i	d	d	l	e	r
s	e	l	b	u	o	d	h	j	e	e
a	d	i	s	a	g	r	e	e	l	v
s	b	e	x	a	m	p	l	e	t	o
t	v	s	d	i	s	g	u	s	t	c
e	c	s	i	m	p	l	e	o	e	s
r	d	i	s	e	a	s	e	p	n	i
x	t	n	i	o	p	p	a	s	i	d
z	a	u	g	m	o	v	e	i	k	o
d	i	s	t	r	a	c	t	d	l	p

Small Words

4. Write the list word that contains these small words.

(a) sag _____

(b) us _____

(c) sea _____

(d) act _____

Revision Words

simple

double

particle

example

twiddle

nettle

Alphabetical Order

5. Write these words in alphabetical order.

move   dispose   disgust   simple

(a) _____

(b) _____

(c) _____

(d) _____

Word Hunt

6. (a) Which three words have a double consonant?

_____ _____ _____

(b) Which list word ends with two vowels? _____

(c) Which two words have one syllable? _____ _____

(d) Which word is the name of a plant? _____

List Words	Practise	Practise	D
reply			
rely			
recall			
resent			
react			
reject			
relation			
review			
try			
kind			

Antonyms

1. Find a list word with an opposite meaning.

(a) nasty _____

(b) ask _____

(c) accept _____

(d) forget _____

Rhyming Words

2. Choose a rhyming word from the list.

(a) nation _____

(b) mind _____

(c) collect _____

(d) subtract _____

Revision Words

crackle

doodle

couple

Bible

taste

uncle

Word Worm

3. Use every third letter to make two list words.

v b r g h e s d j l k e w s c a t t p a t d r r f g y

Difficult words I have found	Practise	Practise

Unit 13

4. Use list and revision words to solve the crossword.

Across

2. Respond.
4. Scribble.
7. Your aunt is one.
8. Throw out.
10. Depend on.
11. Caring.
12. Attempt.

Down

1. Pair.
2. Dislike.
3. One kind of noise.
5. A holy book.
6. Your aunt's husband.
7. Answer.
8. Go over.
9. Sample.
10. Remember.

Memory Master

5. Cover the list and revision words. Write two from memory.

_____ _____

Write a sentence for each word.

(a) _____

(b) _____

Secret Code

6. Use the secret code to find out the list or revision word.

(a) __ __ __ __ __
   2 6 2 8 5

(b) __ __ __ __ __
   13 9 3 8 5

(c) __ __ __ __
   7 6 9 4

a	b	c	d	e	i	k	l	n	r	s	t	u	v	w
1	2	3	4	5	6	7	8	9	10	11	12	13	14	15

List Words	Practise	Practise	D
prepare			
predict			
prefer			
pretend			
prefect			
present			
prevent			
precise			
hand			
picture			

Adding Endings

1. Add 'able' to these words.

   (a) depend   dependable

   (b) predict   _____

   (c) present   _____

   (d) prefer   _____

   (e) prevent   _____

Small Words

2. Write the list word that contains these small words.

   (a) ten   _____

   (b) is   _____

   (c) are   _____

   (d) eve   _____

   (e) red   _____

Difficult words I have found	Practise	Practise

3. Find these list and revision words in the word search.

prepare	predict
prefer	pretend
prefect	present
prevent	precise
hand	picture
muddle	kettle
prickle	needle
table	check

p	d	p	r	i	c	k	l	e	j	t
e	p	r	e	s	e	n	t	k	h	a
l	s	e	s	i	c	e	r	p	g	b
d	a	d	k	e	t	t	l	e	c	l
e	q	i	h	j	n	p	b	l	h	e
e	w	c	a	k	p	r	e	f	e	r
n	e	t	n	e	v	e	r	p	c	a
m	u	d	d	l	e	f	v	z	k	p
o	r	f	h	l	m	e	c	x	f	e
i	t	e	r	u	t	c	i	p	d	r
u	y	g	p	r	e	t	e	n	d	p

All Mixed Up

4. Unjumble the list words.

(a) t e n p e r d _____

(b) t u r i c e p _____

(c) p e r r e f _____

(d) p a r e e r p _____

Synonyms

5. Find a list word with a similar meaning.

(a) gift _____

(b) image _____

(c) foretell _____

(d) stop _____

(e) exact _____

Proof-reading

6. Circle the incorrect words and rewrite them on the lines.

(a) The perfect/prefect was very precise/presice.

_____   _____

(b) I wrote a check/cheque for the picture/pitcher.

_____   _____

Revision Words

muddle	check
kettle	prickle
needle	table

bar   barr

List Words	Practise	Practise	D
barber			
bargain			
barbecue			
barb			
barrel			
barrister			
barrack			
barrier			
again			
change			

Missing Letters

1. Complete the list word.

   (a) __ h __ __ g __

   (b) __ __ __ __ __ l

   (c) __ __ __ __

   (d) __ __ __ b __ c __ e

   (e) __ a __ g __ __ __

   (f) __ g __ __ n

Word Challenge

2. Make as many words as you can from letters in this word.

   barrister

   _____

   _____

   _____

   _____

hatch

cycle

bubble

bottle

buckle

pickle

Difficult words I have found	Practise	Practise

My Spelling Workbook Book D

3. Use list and revision words to solve the crossword.

Across

2. Fizz.
5. Heckle.
7. He cuts men's hair.
10. A covered opening in a wall or floor.
11. Outdoor cooking.
14. Water butt.
15. Alter.
16. Preserve in vinegar.

Down

1. Obstacle.
3. Fasten a belt.
4. Solicitor.
6. Good buy.
8. Sting.
9. A glass container.
12. Once more.
13. Short for bicycle.

Letters into Words

4. Write four list words using the letters on the barrel.

_____

_____

_____

_____

g e
b
r
n
b i a
a r

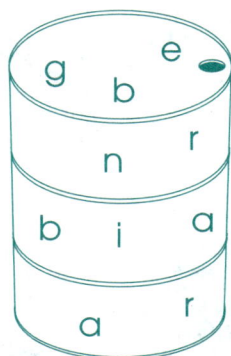

Changing Words

5. Change one letter in each word to make a list or revision word.

(a) garb _____

(b) charge _____

(c) barter _____

(d) tickle _____

Mixed Up Sentences

6. Unjumble the sentences.

(a) from barrel. the the bottle Fill _____

(b) the change to Ask hairstyle. barber your

_____

List Words	Practise	Practise	D
airport			
classroom			
shoelace			
afternoon			
playground			
rainbow			
underground			
football			
off			
engage			

Small Words

1. Write the list word that contains these small words.

   (a) hoe   _____

   (b) lay   _____

   (c) in   _____

   (d) no   _____

   (e) of   _____

Revision Words

pimple

grumble

match

caste

bicycle

settle

Compound Words

2. Add the missing part of the list word.

   (a) _____lace

   (b) after_____

   (c) _____bow

   (d) _____room

Difficult words I have found	Practise	Practise

3. Find these list and revision words in the word search.

airport   classroom

shoelace   afternoon

playground   rainbow

underground   football

off   engage

pimple   grumble

match   caste

bicycle   settle

p	e	l	c	y	c	i	b	d	f	u
o	m	q	g	r	u	m	b	l	e	n
n	o	o	n	r	e	t	f	a	n	d
f	o	o	t	b	a	l	l	s	g	e
i	r	w	t	w	o	b	n	i	a	r
m	s	e	r	e	t	s	a	c	g	g
a	s	h	o	e	l	a	c	e	e	r
t	a	r	p	i	m	p	l	e	g	o
c	l	t	r	o	f	f	a	i	b	u
h	c	y	i	e	l	t	t	e	s	n
u	p	l	a	y	g	r	o	u	n	d

Secret Words

4. (a) Change 'ground' to 'room' in

playground. _____

(b) Change 'foot' to 'net' in football.

_____

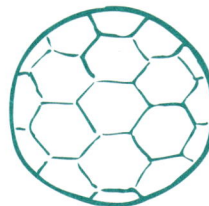

(c) Change 'port' to 'line' in airport.

_____

Alphabetical Order

5. Write these words in alphabetical order.

grumble   afternoon

off   airport

(a) _____

(b) _____

(c) _____

(d) _____

Missing Words

6. Complete using one of these list or revision words.

> afternoon   football   off   playground   rainbow   airport

(a) They played _____ in the _____.

(b) I saw a _____ in the sky this _____.

(c) They came _____ the plane and walked through the

_____.

Revision Unit 3

List Words	Practise	Practise	D
home			
read			
again			
friend			
different			
move			
kind			
picture			
change			
engage			

All Mixed Up

1. Unjumble these revision words.

    (a) i n a g a _____

    (b) t r u p i c e _____

    (c) d e n i r f _____

    (d) h e n a c g _____

    (e) a g g e e n _____

    (f) d i n k _____

Small Words

2. Find smaller words in these words.

    (a) again _____

    _____

    (b) friend _____

    (c) engage _____

    _____

    (d) home _____

Word Worm

3. Circle four revision words which are written backwards in the word worm.

f g h d n e i r f j k i e g a g n e d w a e r u t c i p l k j d a e r v c w

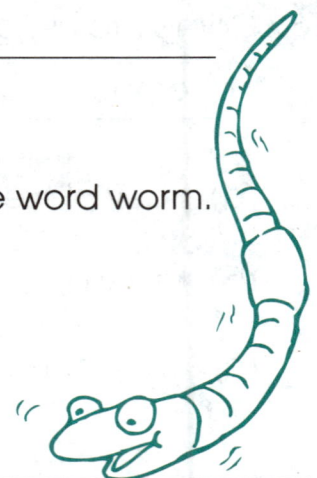

4. Find and circle these words in the story.

engage ✓	different
home	kind
read	picture
again	change
friend	move

I will (engage) my kind friend, to read again, the details under the picture of the different home we want to move to for a change.

Missing Words

5. Complete, using the revision words.

(a) Put a _____ lamp on for a _____.

(b) It would be _____ to help your _____.

(c) _____ the lever to _____ the gear.

(d) Go _____ and _____ your book.

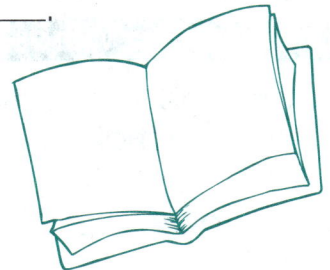

Word Hunt

6. (a) Which two words have a soft 'g'?

_____

_____

(b) Which word has three syllables?

_____

(c) Which word can be present or past tense?

_____

List Words	Practise	Practise	D
guide			
guard			
guess			
guitar			
guilt			
guest			
tongue			
vague			
spell			
air			

Changing Words

1. Change one letter in each word to make a list word.

    (a) glide _____

    (b) value _____

    (c) spill _____

Rhyming Words

2. Choose a rhyming word from the list.

    (a) wide _____

    (b) hard _____

    (c) quilt _____

    (d) hung _____

Revision Words

wriggle

divide

depart

disappoint

rely

pretend

Word Worm

3. Use every third letter to make two list words.

r e t g h o l k n g h g r e u t f e d s g t h u j k i l o l o p t v b

Difficult words I have found	Practise	Practise

4. Use list and revision words to solve the crossword.

Across

3. Fault.
4. Steer.
5. Musical instrument.
8. Imagine.
10. Depend.
12. Let down.
13. Squirm.
14. Unclear.

Down

1. Separate.
2. Watch carefully.
5. Estimate.
6. Visitor.
7. Name letters in a word.
9. Leave.
11. It is in your mouth.
15. It is all around us.

5. Use the secret code to find out the list or revision word.

(a) __ __ __ __ __
   4 12 5 2 3

(b) __ __ __ __ __
   10 8 3 6 6

(c) __ __ __ __ __
   4 12 5 6 11

(d) __ __ __ __ __ __
   2 3 8 1 9 11

(e) __ __ __ __ __ __ __
   8 9 3 11 3 7 2

a	d	e	g	i	l	n	p	r	s	t	u
1	2	3	4	5	6	7	8	9	10	11	12

Proof-reading

6. Circle the correct words and rewrite them on the lines.

(a) We will have to really/rely on the gide/guide to get there.

_____   _____

(b) I do not like to dissappoint/disappoint my guest/guessed.

_____   _____

List Words	Practise	Practise	D
knot			
knee			
knife			
knight			
knack			
knit			
knock			
knuckle			
away			
animal			

Letters into Words

1. Write five list words using the letters on the knee.

_____

_____

_____

_____

_____

h k t i c g n k o a

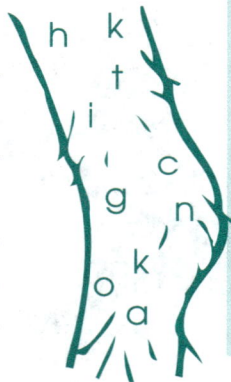

Revision Words

football

barb

toggle

millimetre

descend

disease

Word Meanings

2. Match the words to their meanings.

(a) knock •   • finger joint

(b) animal •   • blade

(c) knuckle •   • rap

(d) knife •   • creature

Difficult words I have found	Practise	Practise

3. Find these list and revision words in the word search.

knot   knee

knock   knife

knight   knack

knit   knuckle

away   animal

football   barb

toggle   millimetre

descend   disease

e	k	g	f	n	k	n	a	c	k	l
w	n	y	a	w	a	m	z	b	n	k
m	i	l	l	i	m	e	t	r	e	j
q	f	h	d	b	f	n	o	a	e	d
e	e	j	s	v	o	a	n	b	s	e
l	b	k	k	c	o	n	k	a	a	s
k	r	l	n	c	t	i	x	s	e	c
c	t	p	i	x	b	m	c	d	s	e
u	y	o	g	z	a	a	v	f	i	n
n	u	i	h	a	l	l	b	g	d	d
k	n	i	t	e	l	g	g	o	t	h

All Mixed Up

4. Unjumble the list words.

(a) y a w a   _____

(b) g i n t h k   _____

(c) t o n k   _____

(d) c u n k e k l   _____

Word Hunt

5. (a) Which two words name joints?

_____   _____

(b) Which word means the opposite of 'ascend'?

_____

(c) Which two words have a double vowel?

_____   _____

Homophones

6. Circle and write the correct word.

(a) Use a reef knot/not to secure the boat.   _____

(b) The night/knight was away on a crusade.   _____

(c) Can you knit/nit a scarf for the snowman?   _____

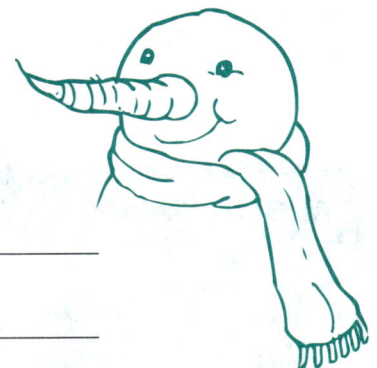

List Words	Practise	Practise	D
gnat			
gnaw			
foreign			
gnome			
gnash			
gnarled			
campaign			
assign			
house			
point			

Word Challenge

1. Make as many words as you can from letters in this word.

   campaign

   _____

   _____

   _____

   _____

Missing Letters

2. Complete the list word and write it.

   (a) __ o __ e i __ __   _____

   (b) p __ __ __ t   _____

   (c) __ s s __ __ __   _____

   (d) __ __ __ m __   _____

   (e) __ n __ __ h   _____

   (f) g __ __ t   _____

Difficult words I have found	Practise	Practise

3. Use list and revision words to solve the crossword.

Across

1. Increase.
7. Dislike.
9. Crusade.
10. From overseas.
13. A small insect.
14. Grind.
15. Home.

Down

2. The thin sharp end of something.
3. A good price.
4. Allocate.
5. Make ready.
6. We fly from here.
8. Spout.
11. Knobbly.
12. Chew.
14. A small funny figure.

Change the Tense

4. Change the tense of the list words.

	Present	Past
(a)	gnash	gnashed
(b)	point	_____
(c)	assign	_____
(d)	gnaw	_____

Revision Words

resent	prepare	airport
bargain	nozzle	multiply

Mixed Up Sentences

5. Unjumble the sentences.

(a) had for prepare The the campaign. knight to

_____

_____

_____

(b) leave to to airport holiday. We the foreign our went for

_____

_____

List Words	Practise	Practise	D
whole			
wrap			
wrist			
wreck			
wrong			
wrestle			
wring			
wrinkle			
page			
letter			

Changing Words

1. Change one letter in each word to make a list word.

   (a) while _____

   (b) litter _____

   (c) bring _____

Revision Words

decide

discover

recall

prefer

giggle

shoelace

Alphabetical Order

2. Write these words in alphabetical order.

   wrap   wring   letter   whole

   (a) _____

   (b) _____

   (c) _____

   (d) _____

Difficult words I have found	Practise	Practise	

3. Find these list and revision words in the word search.

whole	wrap
wrist	wreck
wrong	wrestle
wring	wrinkle
page	letter
decide	discover
recall	prefer
giggle	shoelace

w	w	s	l	p	e	w	w	e	l	g
r	r	d	w	r	i	n	k	l	e	b
e	i	f	k	o	r	q	c	d	t	n
s	n	d	e	c	i	d	e	c	t	w
t	g	i	g	g	l	e	r	v	e	r
l	t	s	i	r	w	a	w	f	r	a
e	a	c	j	l	l	a	c	e	r	p
m	z	o	h	i	t	z	s	l	t	a
n	x	v	g	u	y	w	r	o	n	g
b	c	e	c	a	l	e	o	h	s	e
v	p	r	e	f	e	r	x	w	r	h

Synonyms

4. Find a list word with a similar meaning.

(a) crease _____

(b) intact _____

(c) mistaken _____

(d) ruin _____

(e) struggle _____

Missing Words

5. Complete using list or revision words.

(a) I can't read the third _____ of the _____.

(b) You need to _____ which colour you _____.

(c) I will _____ the bandage round your _____.

Homophones

6. Circle the correct word.

(a) Wrap/Rap the wrap/rap CD in tissue paper.

(b) Wring/Ring out the wet towel before you wring/ring your mum.

List Words	Practise	Practise	D
rhyme			
rhapsody			
rhythm			
ghastly			
rhombus			
rhubarb			
vehicle			
ghost			
mother			
answer			

Small Words

1. Write the list word that contains these small words.

   (a) has _____

   (b) bus _____

   (c) an _____

Revision Words

barrel

detach

disagree

react

prevent

barber

All Mixed Up

2. Unjumble the list words.

   (a) t h a s l y g _____

   (b) t h o g s _____

   (c) h o r m s u b _____

   (d) s h o p d a r y _____

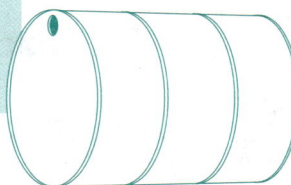

Difficult words I have found	Practise	Practise

3. Use list and revision words to solve the crossword.

Across

1. A plant with long red stems.
6. Bliss.
9. A car or lorry.
10. Argue.
12. He cuts hair.
14. Respond to.
15. Beat.

Down

2. Cask.
3. Female parent.
4. Phantom.
5. Poem.
7. Stop.
8. Reply.
10. Separate.
11. Extremely horrible.
13. A shape.

Secret Code

4. Use the secret code to find out the list or revision word.

(a) __ __ __ __ __
   6 7 10 12 13

(b) __ __ __ __ __
   11 5 1 3 13

(c) __ __ __ __ __
   11 7 15 9 5

(d) __ __ __ __ __ __ __
   11 7 10 9 2 14 12

(e) __ __ __ __ __ __ __ __
   4 8 12 1 6 11 5 5

a	b	c	d	e	g	h	i	m	o	r	s	t	u	y
1	2	3	4	5	6	7	8	9	10	11	12	13	14	15

Word Worm

5. Use every third letter to make two list words.

c h m y j o y r t w e h q q a e t y r o p r o u h n k y l v m s l e d f

List Words	Practise	Practise	D
lamb			
comb			
climb			
thumb			
crumb			
numb			
dumb			
doubt			
found			
study			

Rhyming Words

1. Choose a rhyming word from the list.

   (a) home _____

   (b) shout _____

   (c) round _____

Word Hunt

2. (a) Which word names a digit?

   _____

   (b) Which word rhymes with 'cram'?

   _____

   (c) Which two words have an 'ou' pattern in them?

   _____ _____

Revision Words

playground	guzzle	pentagon
declare	reply	present

Difficult words I have found	Practise	Practise

3. Find these list and revision words in the word search.

lamb	comb
climb	thumb
crumb	numb
dumb	doubt
found	study
playground	guzzle
pentagon	declare
reply	present

m	y	d	e	c	l	a	r	e	c	s
e	l	z	z	u	g	s	x	s	f	d
n	p	b	p	e	n	t	a	g	o	n
b	e	m	j	k	y	u	z	w	u	u
c	r	u	m	b	u	d	a	e	n	o
l	z	d	h	m	i	y	q	d	d	r
i	x	a	n	u	m	b	c	c	n	g
m	c	s	g	h	o	t	o	v	b	y
b	v	d	f	t	p	r	m	f	g	a
t	n	e	s	e	r	p	b	m	a	l
d	o	u	b	t	l	e	w	r	t	p

Mixed Up Sentences

4. Unjumble the sentences.

(a) mountain. shepherd was lamb The that the lost on found the

_____

maa-aa!

(b) whole no juice! doubt that could There's guzzle the bottle of he

_____

Letters into Words

5. Write three list words using the letters on the lamb.

_____

_____

_____

Magic Words

6. Change the first word into the last by changing one letter on each line to make a new word.

Example:

rash	(a) comb	(b) dumb
lash	_____	_____
last	_____	_____
past	lame	lamp

List Words	Practise	Practise	D
calm			
palm			
balm			
qualm			
salmon			
calf			
yolk			
chalk			
still			
learn			

Missing Letters

1. Complete the list word and write it.

(a) __ h __ __ k   _____

(b) __ a __ __ o __   _____

(c) __ u __ __ __   _____

(d) l __ __ __ __   _____

(e) __ __ i __ __   _____

(f) __ o __ __   _____

Alphabetical Order

2. Write these words in alphabetical order

chalk   calf   balm   calm

(a) _____

(b) _____

(c) _____

(d) _____

Difficult words I have found	Practise	Practise

3. Use list and revision words to solve the crossword.

Across

1. Foretell.
5. This is round.
7. A baby cow.
8. A type of tree.
9. A type of fish.
11. Throw out.
12. The yellow of an egg.
14. Not moving.

Down

2. Refuse.
3. Lotion.
4. Room in a school.
5. You write on a board with this.
6. A small wave.
7. Peaceful.
10. Discover.
13. Doubt.

Secret Words

4. (a) Change 'lm' to 'ke' in qualm. _____

     (b) Change 'mon' to 't' in salmon. _____

     (c) Change 'i' to 'a' in still. _____

Describing Words

5. Write the correct noun.
Draw the picture these adjectives describe.

(a) splashing, scaly   (b) tall, leafy

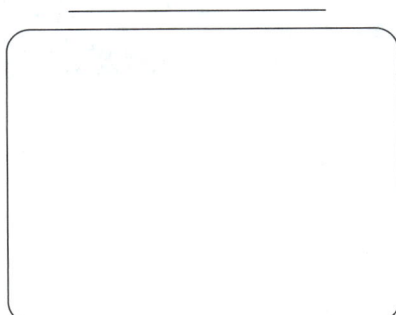  

Revision Words
predict
reject
classroom
ripple
circle
decline

List Words	Practise	Practise	D
castle			
listen			
fasten			
whistle			
thistle			
Christmas			
bristle			
glisten			
should			
America			

Small Words

1. Write the list word that contains these small words.

   (a) me _____

   (b) cast_____

   (c) this _____

Revision Words

- disaster
- relation
- precise
- afternoon
- subtract
- dispose

Word Challenge

2. Make as many words as you can from letters in this word.

Christmas

_____

_____

_____

_____

Difficult words I have found	Practise	Practise

3. Find these list and revision words in the word search.

castle	listen
fasten	whistle
thistle	Christmas
bristle	glisten
should	America
disaster	relation
precise	afternoon
subtract	dispose

C	h	r	i	s	t	m	a	s	s	e	e
c	e	c	g	x	p	n	o	h	u	w	l
a	l	v	l	z	l	o	p	o	b	s	t
s	t	f	i	a	k	i	r	u	t	x	s
t	s	a	s	s	j	t	e	l	r	r	i
l	i	s	t	e	n	a	c	d	a	e	h
e	h	t	e	d	h	l	i	w	c	t	t
b	w	e	n	f	g	e	s	e	t	s	d
n	v	n	o	o	n	r	e	t	f	a	c
m	d	i	s	p	o	s	e	r	q	s	v
a	c	i	r	e	m	A	i	t	a	i	f
b	r	i	s	t	l	e	u	y	z	d	r

Word Meanings

4. Match the words to their meanings.

(a) glisten •   • fortress

(b) castle •   • secure

(c) fasten •   • shrill noise

(d) whistle •   • sparkle

Missing Words

5. Complete using one of the list or revision words.

(a) You _____ be

_____ when adding up.

(b) A _____ of mine lives in

_____.

(c) They had to _____ of the

rubble after the _____.

Memory Master

6. Cover the list and revision words. Write two from memory.

_____   _____

Write a sentence for each word.

(a) _____

(b) _____

Revision Unit 4

List Words	Practise	Practise	D
house			
should			
learn			
answer			
spell			
animal			
point			
letter			
mother			
found			

All Mixed Up

1. Unjumble these revision words.

(a) h o r m e t _____

(b) h u l o d s _____

(c) u n d o f _____

(d) l e p s l _____

(e) r e s w a n _____

(f) p i n t o _____

(g) n i l a m a _____

(h) e n l r a _____

Word Worm

2. Circle four revision words which are written backwards in the word worm.

3. Find and circle these words in the story.

should ✓	spell
answer	letter
point	learn
found	animal
house	mother

I (should) like to point out in my letter that my mother is happy for me to keep the animal I found outside our house for a short spell. However, she would like an answer to learn when you will pick it up.

Missing Words

4. Complete, using the revision words.

(a) She did not _____ the _____.

(b) _____ out the mayor's _____.

(c) I have _____ it difficult to _____ about astrology.

(d) My _____ was confined to hospital for a _____.

Small Words

5. Find smaller words in these words.

(a) learn _____ _____

(b) point _____

(c) mother _____ _____

_____ _____ _____

Word Hunt

6. (a) Which words have an 'ou' pattern? _____ _____

_____

(b) Which word has a silent 'w'? _____

(c) Which words have double consonants? _____ _____

List Words	Practise	Practise	D
I'm			
don't			
I'll			
we'll			
can't			
wasn't			
didn't			
he's			
world			
clean			

Whole Words

1. Write the contractions in words.

(a) I'll _____

(b) he's _____

(c) wasn't _____

(d) I'm _____

Antonyms

2. Find a list word with an opposite meaning.

(a) can _____

(b) did _____

(c) dirty _____

(d) do _____

Revision Words
guide knock gnome wrist rhythm lamb

Difficult words I have found	Practise	Practise

3. Use list and revision words to solve the crossword.

Across

2. Short for he is.
3. At the top of your hand.
4. Small funny figure.
5. Short for I am.
8. Short for cannot.
9. Short for we will.
10. Globe.
12. Baby sheep.
13. Short for do not.

Down

1. Beat.
4. Steer.
6. Rap.
7. Short for I will.
8. Not dirty.
9. Short for was not.
11. Short for did not.

Mixed Up Sentences

4. Unjumble the sentences.

(a) keep clean. My can't room his brother

_____

(b) lamb I'm mint and dinner for having sauce tonight.

_____

Proof-reading

5. Circle the correct words.

(a) He did'nt/didn't know the world/wurld was round.

(b) Be careful or you'll nock/knock the gnome/nome over.

List Words	Practise	Practise	D
mistake			
mischief			
mislead			
misfit			
misfire			
mislay			
mishap			
misplace			
Edinburgh			
London			

All Mixed Up

1. Unjumble the list words.

   (a) g r u b d i n E h _____

   (b) c h i m f i e s _____

   (c) e l d a s i m _____

   (d) a s l i m y _____

Revision Words

salmon

whistle

guess

glisten

gnat

wrong

Secret Words

2. (a) Change 'mis' to 're' in misplace.

   _____

   (b) Change 'mis' to 'de' in mislay.

   _____

   (c) Change 'Lo' to 'aba' in London.

   _____

Difficult words I have found	Practise	Practise

3. Find these list and revision words in the word search.

mistake	mischief
mislead	misfit
misfire	mislay
mishap	misplace
Edinburgh	London
salmon	whistle
guess	glisten
gnat	wrong

f	b	g	v	m	i	s	t	a	k	E
e	n	n	c	s	d	h	i	o	i	d
i	L	o	n	d	o	n	f	p	u	i
h	p	r	x	a	f	g	s	l	y	n
c	a	w	e	l	t	s	i	h	w	b
s	h	y	a	l	s	i	m	n	t	u
i	s	g	u	e	s	s	j	o	r	r
m	i	s	l	e	a	d	k	m	e	g
m	m	z	n	e	t	s	i	l	g	h
m	i	s	p	l	a	c	e	a	w	q
t	a	n	g	e	r	i	f	s	i	m

Synonyms

4. Find a list word with a similar meaning.

(a) deceive _____

(b) accident _____

(c) error _____

(d) prank _____

(e) lose _____

Rhyming Words

5. Choose a rhyming word from the list or revision words.

(a) decay _____

(b) indeed _____

(c) belief _____

(d) song _____

(e) hat _____

(f) bristle _____

Secret Code

6. Use the secret code to find the list or revision word.

(a) ___ ___ ___ ___ ___
  15 12 11 10 5

(b) ___ ___ ___ ___ ___ ___
  13 1 8 9 11 10

(c) ___ ___ ___ ___ ___ ___
  9 7 13 4 7 14

(d) ___ ___ ___ ___ ___ ___ ___
  15 6 7 13 14 8 3

(e) ___ ___ ___ ___ ___ ___ ___
  9 7 13 8 3 1 2

a	d	e	f	g	h	i	l	m	n	o	r	s	t	w
1	2	3	4	5	6	7	8	9	10	11	12	13	14	15

List Words	Practise	Practise	D
pigeon			
geology			
geometry			
geography			
weather			
weapon			
weave			
wealth			
Dublin			
Rome			

Alphabetical Order

1. Write these words in alphabetical order.

weapon   weather
weave   wealth

(a) _____

(b) _____

(c) _____

(d) _____

Revision Words

rhapsody

climb

chalk

castle

guilt

knack

Letters into Words

2. Write three list words using the letters on the triangle.

_____

_____

_____

r
l   g
e
y   m   y
t   o   e   g   a

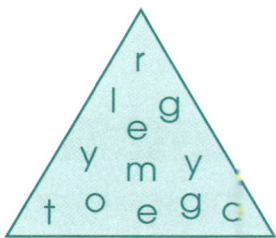

Difficult words I have found	Practise	Practise

3. Use list and revision words to solve the crossword.

Across

1. To go up.
3. Flair.
5. Intertwine.
6. Italy's capital city.
7. Fortune.
10. Fortress.
11. This could harm someone.
13. Blame.
14. The study of places.

Down

1. Something to write on a board with.
2. A branch of mathematics.
4. Republic of Ireland's capital city.
6. A state of bliss.
8. It could be sunny or rainy.
9. The study of rocks.
12. A type of bird.

Missing Letters

4. Complete the list word and write it.

(a) __ o __ e   _____

(b) g __ __ g __ __ p __ __   _____

(c) __ u __ __ i __   _____

(d) __ e a __ __ n   _____

(e) __ __ __ v __   _____

Word Hunt

5. (a) Which two words name cities?

_____ _____

(b) Which four words end with a 'y'?

_____ _____

_____ _____

(c) Which word names a bird?

_____

Word Worm

6. Circle four words which are written backwards in the word worm.

List Words	Practise	Practise	D
antibody			
antibiotic			
antiseptic			
antidote			
cooperate			
coordinate			
copilot			
co-star			
Paris			
Madrid			

Small Words

1. Write the list word that contains these small words.

(a) lot _____

(b) tar _____

(c) rid _____

Revision Words

assign

rhubarb

crumb

fasten

gnarled

wreck

Word Challenge

2. Make as many words as you can from letters in this word.

antiseptic

_____

_____

_____

_____

Difficult words I have found	Practise	Practise

3. Find these list and revision words in the word search.

antibody	antibiotic
antidote	antiseptic
cooperate	coordinate
copilot	co-star
Paris	Madrid
assign	rhubarb
crumb	fasten
gnarled	wreck

c	i	t	p	e	s	i	t	n	a	f
o	a	n	t	i	d	o	t	e	g	d
o	q	c	r	u	M	b	o	n	h	s
p	y	n	g	n	a	r	l	e	d	a
e	d	g	t	y	d	a	i	t	j	w
r	o	i	r	u	r	b	p	s	k	r
a	b	s	e	i	i	u	o	a	l	e
t	i	s	w	o	d	h	c	f	p	c
e	t	a	n	i	d	r	o	o	c	k
a	n	t	i	b	i	o	t	i	c	z
r	a	t	s	o	c	P	a	r	i	s

Change the Tense

4. Change the tense of the list words.

Present	Past
(a) assign	assigned
(b) co-star	_____
(c) cooperate	_____
(d) coordinate	_____

Word Worm

5. Cross out every second letter. The leftover letters will make three list or revision words.

Missing Words

6. Complete using one of the list or revision words.

(a) The _____ rushed the _____ to the disaster area.

(b) The _____ would not _____ with the director.

(c) _____ your seat belt before driving that _____ of a car!

(d) _____ and _____ are both capital cities.

List Words	Practise	Practise	D
non-stop			
non-fiction			
nonsense			
non-stick			
non-slip			
non-returnable			
non-event			
non-starter			
Berlin			
Moscow			

Mirror Writing

1. Write the mirror written words correctly.

   (a) Berlin   _____

   (b) nonsense   _____

   (c) non-stop   _____

All Mixed Up

2. Unjumble the list words.

   (a) n e t - n o v e n _____

   (b) k i t - c o n s n _____

   (c) o M s w o c _____

   (d) r a t - r e s t o n n _____

Revision Words

guard	knife	campaign
wrinkle	ghost	dumb

Difficult words I have found	Practise	Practise	

3. Use list and revision words to solve the crossword.

Across

2. Without stopping.
3. Cut with this.
5. It won't stick.
7. Unable to talk.
9. Phantom.
11. He fails to start the race.
14. You cannot take it back.
15. A line on an old face.

Down

1. Fact.
4. The capital of Russia.
6. Watch closely.
8. The capital of Germany.
10. Crusade.
11. A very unsuccessful occasion.
12. Rubbish.
13. Not slippery.

Secret Code

4. Use the secret code to find out the list or revision word.

(a) __ __ __ __ __
   6 9 5 4 3

(b) __ __ __ __ __ __
   8 10 12 2 10 13

(c) __ __ __ __ __ __
   1 3 11 7 5 9

(d) __ __ __ __ __ __ __
  13 11 5 9 6 7 3

(e) __ __ __ __ __ __ __ __
   9 10 9 12 3 9 12 3

b	c	e	f	i	k	l	m	n	o	r	s	w
1	2	3	4	5	6	7	8	9	10	11	12	13

Missing Letters

5. Complete the list or revision word.

(a) __ __ __ - __ __ i __

(b) __ __ __ __ - __ __ o __

(c) __ __ m __

List Words	Practise	Practise	D
marshes			
foxes			
lunches			
churches			
babies			
ladies			
lorries			
skies			
Europe			
great			

Changing Words

1. Change one letter in each word to make a list word.

   (a) punches _____

   (b) skids _____

   (c) marches _____

Revision Words

listen	palm	guitar
knee	wrap	ghastly

Singular Nouns

2. Write the singular of these plural list words.

Plural	Singular
(a) lorries	lorry
(b) babies	_____
(c) ladies	_____
(d) skies	_____

Difficult words I have found	Practise	Practise

3. Find these list and revision words in the word search.

marshes   foxes

lunches   churches

babies   ladies

lorries   skies

Europe   great

listen   palm

guitar   knee

wrap   ghastly

q	l	k	g	f	t	y	g	f	x	s
t	a	e	r	g	r	u	e	e	n	k
w	p	p	n	d	s	p	a	l	m	i
g	o	o	e	s	e	i	b	a	b	e
h	i	r	t	s	h	i	h	d	g	s
a	u	u	s	a	c	f	j	i	u	e
s	s	E	i	r	r	o	l	e	i	h
t	y	p	l	q	u	x	k	s	t	c
l	m	a	r	s	h	e	s	d	a	n
y	t	r	h	w	c	s	l	s	r	u
e	r	w	j	e	r	o	p	a	z	l

Describing Words

4. Write the correct noun. Draw the picture these adjectives describe.

(a) large, stone, tall

(b) crying, squirming

_____

_____

Letters into Words

5. Write three list words using the letters on the sandwich.

_____

_____

_____

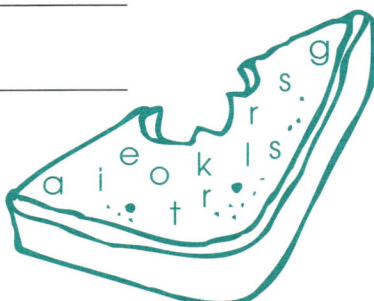

Magic Words

6. Change the first word into the last by changing one letter on each line to make a new word.

Example:

palm	(a) foxes	(b) wrap
pale	_____	_____
sale	_____	_____
sane	cones	grip

List Words	Practise	Practise	D
everyone			
everybody			
anyone			
no-one			
nobody			
someone			
anything			
somebody			
Cardiff			
Belfast			

Compound Words

1. Add the missing part of the list word.

(a) _____thing

(b) every_____

(c) _____one

(d) some_____

(e) any_____

Alphabetical Order

2. Write these words in alphabetical order.

no-one   someone   nobody   somebody

(a) _____ (b) _____

(c) _____ (d) _____

Revision Words		
thumb	thistle	guest
knot	wrestle	rhyme

Difficult words I have found	Practise	Practise

3. Use list and revision words to solve the crossword.

Across

1. You can tie this.
3. A thorny plant.
6. Another word for 'one person'.
11. Another word for 'all the people'.
13. Capital of Wales.
15. Another word for 'not one person'.
16. Visitor.

Down

2. A digit on your hand.
4. Any person.
5. Capital of Northern Ireland.
7. Not one person.
8. All the people.
9. Struggle.
10. Any object.
12. One person.
14. Poem.

Secret Words

4. (a) Change 'body' to 'times' in somebody. _____

   (b) Change 'one' to 'where' in everyone. _____

   (c) Change 'diff' to 'avan' in Cardiff. _____

Word Worm Anagram

5. Choose every third letter and then rearrange them to make a list word.

List Words	Practise	Practise	D
stated			
replied			
asked			
yelled			
shouted			
cried			
demanded			
exclaimed			
Italy			
Switzerland			

Small Words

1. Write the list word that contains these small words.

(a) man _____

(b) lie _____

(c) ate _____

(d) out _____

Revision Words

numb

calm

Christmas

tongue

knit

rhombus

Word Challenge

2. Make as many words as you can from letters in this word.

demanded

_____

_____

_____

_____

Difficult words I have found	Practise	Practise

3. Find these list and revision words in the word search.

stated	replied
asked	yelled
shouted	cried
demanded	exclaimed
Italy	Switzerland
numb	calm
Christmas	tongue
knit	rhombus

S	a	m	t	s	i	r	h	C	c	d
w	d	d	e	l	l	e	y	x	v	e
i	e	e	q	o	p	p	l	z	b	m
t	i	m	w	i	y	l	a	t	l	a
z	r	i	e	u	d	i	k	o	s	n
e	c	a	l	m	e	e	j	n	u	d
r	k	l	d	y	t	d	h	g	b	e
l	n	c	e	n	u	m	b	u	m	d
a	i	x	k	t	o	j	g	e	o	n
n	t	e	s	r	h	k	f	a	h	m
d	e	t	a	t	s	l	d	s	r	f

Memory Master

4. Cover the list and revision words. Write two from memory.

_____ _____

Write a sentence for each word.

(a) _____

(b) _____

Change the Tense

5. Complete the table.

(a) state	stating	stated
(b)	replying	
(c) ask		
(d)		demanded

Rhyming Words

6. Choose a rhyming word from the list.

(a) held

_____

(b) sighed

_____

(c) understand

_____

Revision Unit 5

List Words	Practise	Practise	D
world			
great			
Dublin			
Cardiff			
Edinburgh			
London			
Paris			
Moscow			
Europe			
Belfast			

All Mixed Up

1. Unjumble these revision words. Some of the letters may be capitals.

   (a) d r a f f i c _____

   (b) s p a i r _____

   (c) s t e l f a b _____

   (d) b l i n d u _____

   (e) d l o o n n _____

   (f) p e r u o e _____

   (g) d r o w l _____

Word Worm

2. Circle four revision words in the word worm.

bshgreatjiyParisbhmDublingxwEuropejkn

3. Find and circle these words in the story.

great ✔	Dublin
London	Edinburgh
Cardiff	Paris
Europe	Moscow
world	Belfast

There was a (great) debate in London to decide the venue for the next Olympics. Many capital cities in the world were represented including Dublin, Cardiff, Edinburgh, Paris, Belfast and Moscow. However, it was decided to hold them outside Europe.

TO IRELAND

Missing Words

4. Complete, using the revision words.

(a) How far is it from _____ to _____?

(b) _____ and _____ are in different parts of Ireland.

(c) _____ is a _____ place to visit in Russia.

(d) _____ is a continent in the _____.

Small Words

5. Find smaller words in these words.

(a) world _____

(b) great _____ _____

(c) Belfast _____ _____ _____ _____

Word Hunt

6. (a) Which words have five letters? _____ _____

_____

(b) Which word rhymes with fate? _____

(c) Which word has a silent 'g'? _____

My Dictionary Words: Aa to Ii _____

Aa

Bb

Cc

Dd

Ee

Ff

Gg

Hh

Ii

Jj

Kk

Ll

Mn

Nn

Oo

Pp

Qq

Rr

My Dictionary Words: **S** **s** to **Z** **z** _____

Ss	Tt	Uu

Vv	Ww	Xx

Yy	Zz